Original title:
The Frozen World

Copyright © 2024 Swan Charm
All rights reserved.

Author: Johan Kirsipuu
ISBN HARDBACK: 978-9916-79-297-1
ISBN PAPERBACK: 978-9916-79-298-8
ISBN EBOOK: 978-9916-79-299-5

Solstice Secrets

Whispers of light in a sunlit haze,
A dance of shadows through winter's maze.
The longest night holds stories untold,
Ancient secrets in the dark unfold.

Stars weave magic in the frigid air,
Moonlight kisses the world with tender care.
From the depths of darkness, hope will arise,
As dawn breaks gently across the skies.

Arctic Murmurs

In the stillness where the cold winds sigh,
Whispers of ice drift softly by.
The polar night speaks in creaks and groans,
Echoes of solitude in icy tones.

A dance of auroras paints the black dome,
Colors of nature, cold yet home.
Each flake descends with a silent grace,
Leaving soft patterns in this frozen place.

Specter of Snow

Silent shadows on a blanket of white,
The land transformed in the soft twilight.
Ghostly figures glide on frosty air,
Whispers of beauty woven with care.

Footprints vanish, swallowed by the cold,
Each step a story waiting to be told.
Frozen breath mingles with the night,
A symphony played in pale blue light.

Glacial Reflections

In the still waters, the glaciers weep,
Memories trapped in their frozen keep.
Shards of blue and white catch the sun,
Time is a river that's never outrun.

Reflections shimmer with tales of the past,
Moments of beauty that forever last.
The dance of ice speaks a language divine,
In the heart of winter, a story aligns.

Winter's Veil

The world is wrapped in white,
Soft whispers fill the air.
Beneath the starry light,
A hush, a tranquil prayer.

Trees wear coats of ice,
Branches heavy, calm, and still.
Nature's sweet disguise,
Time paused on winter's hill.

Frosted breath on glass,
Painting scenes of pure delight.
Moments gently pass,
In the quiet of the night.

Footsteps crunch on snow,
Echoes of a lonely sound.
Where the chill winds blow,
Magic lingers all around.

Dreams woven with snowflakes,
Falling softly from the sky.
In the stillness, wakes,
A beauty that will never die.

Gleaming Silence

A calm before the storm,
The world holds its breath tight.
Moonlight begins to warm,
The shadows drift to night.

Stars twinkle like fire,
Whispers dance in the trees.
A heart's quiet desire,
Carried softly on the breeze.

Beneath the silent sky,
Time falls gently in place.
As dreams begin to fly,
Wrapped in a cool embrace.

Each moment like a pearl,
Glowing softly in the dark.
Mysteries swirl and twirl,
Leaving just a glowing mark.

In this peaceful expanse,
The night's magic unfolds.
Embrace the night's romance,
In the gleaming silence, behold.

Shimmering Cold

The air is crisp and clear,
Each breath a cloud of mist.
Winter whispers near,
In a world wrapped in bliss.

Icicles hang like glass,
Sparkling in the pale sun.
Time seems slow to pass,
In the chill, joy's begun.

Snowflakes swirl and dance,
Painting all in gentle white.
Nature's timeless trance,
In the embrace of night.

Footprints in the snow,
Lead to secrets untold.
Where the shadows flow,
In the shimmering cold.

A symphony of frost,
Echoing in the skies.
What we cherish most,
Lives on in winter's guise.

Frozen Traces

Along the lonely way,
Markings in the snow lead.
Stories softly say,
Of winter's gentle deed.

Whispers of the past,
Tell of laughter and of cheer.
Memories that last,
In the winter's ambiance near.

Every step a tale,
Captured in the icy ground.
Life's sweet, fleeting trail,
Where our hearts together bound.

Beneath a sky of gray,
Dreams and hopes intertwine.
In the soft decay,
Of time's unyielding line.

Frozen traces remain,
Carved in the heart's own space.
Though the cold may reign,
Love's warmth finds its place.

Tranquility on a Slippery Slope

Gentle winds brush the trees,
Whispers dart through the pines,
Frozen leaves dance on chill air,
Nature's song softly aligns.

Footsteps trace a winding path,
Where peace blends with the frost,
Each breath a fleeting moment,
In silence, we find what's lost.

The world lingers in stillness,
As the sun begins to rise,
Soft hues bleed into shadows,
Life stirs with open eyes.

A glance at the steep descent,
Worries fade with each glide,
Calm settles as I lean back,
Trusting the slope as my guide.

Here, amidst the crisp and clear,
Harmony reigns in this space,
Tranquility's embrace surrounds,
A gentle smile on my face.

Spectacles of Snowflakes

Falling whispers grace the ground,
Delicate crystals swirl and spin,
Each a wonder, unique, profound,
Winter's lace wraps the world in.

Children dance in joyful glee,
Hands outstretched to catch the flakes,
Glistening jewels, pure esprit,
Nature's gift, the earth awakes.

Underneath a canopy,
Soft silence blankets all around,
Heartbeats harmonize with peace,
In this moment, love is found.

As night falls, stars gently gleam,
Reflecting on the snowy bed,
A quiet sense of mystic dream,
While visions of warmth spread.

Wrapped in coats and cozy thoughts,
We drink in the magic's glow,
Each snowflake's tale softly brought,
In winter's grasp, we savor slow.

Shadows on the Glacial Plains

Glistening fields stretch out wide,
Beneath the sun's wavering light,
Imposing giants stand aside,
Casting shadows, dark as night.

Footprints linger in the ice,
Stories etched in the terrain,
Whispers of ancient sacrifice,
A testament to joy and pain.

Echoes bounce from vast horizons,
Where the sun melts into red,
Hints of warmth from the dawn's sons,
Chasing phantoms in my head.

Breezes tease the frosty air,
With tales of the wild and free,
Mirages dance without a care,
Painting dreams for eyes to see.

As twilight descends with grace,
The glacial plains bear their truth,
In shadows cast, we find our place,
Revealing wisdom of our youth.

Echoing in the Cold

In the hush of winter's breath,
Sounds reverberate through the trees,
Echoes of life and fleeting death,
In the chill, a gentle tease.

Voices carry, rich and clear,
Across the stillness, winds unite,
The world listens, sharp and near,
Each note a spark in the night.

Fires crackle in the gloam,
Eager tales of time unfold,
While we seek our spirits' home,
In the warmth, memories told.

Stars wink from the fabric of dark,
Whispered lullabies fill the air,
In the night, our souls embark,
Echoing dreams laid bare.

Here, in cold, we find our peace,
Cocooned in the embrace of night,
With every echo, hearts release,
The beauty of this timeless rite.

A Winter's Solitude

In the hush of snow's embrace,
The world is draped in white lace.
Whispers of the cold wind sigh,
Beneath the gray, the silence lies.

Frosted branches gleam like stars,
While shadows cling to moonlit cars.
A stillness deep, a tranquil peace,
In winter's grasp, my thoughts release.

The fire crackles soft and low,
As falling flakes begin to grow.
Coffee steams in morning light,
A moment's warmth in endless night.

Birds take flight, their songs are rare,
Through the chill, they roam the air.
Each flake a tale, each gust a dream,
In solitude, the heart can gleam.

Fingers trace the window's frost,
Memories linger, never lost.
In every hush, the soul can find,
A world reborn, both fierce and kind.

Shivering Reveries

In twilight's chill, my thoughts set free,
Drifting along like leaves from a tree.
Each breath a mist in the frosty air,
In shivering dreams, I wander there.

Gentle moonlight, a silver glance,
Awakens hope, ignites romance.
Through shadows deep, my spirit flows,
In every whisper, the winter knows.

Echoes of laughter, far away,
In the stillness, they softly sway.
A tapestry of snow and sky,
Each moment fleeting, a soft goodbye.

Crimson leaves in icy hands,
Painting visions of distant lands.
A fleeting warmth beneath the cold,
In shivering reveries, I unfold.

Reality fades, the heart takes flight,
Transforming dusk into soft light.
In icy breath, my hopes arise,
A dance of dreams beneath the skies.

Glimmering Icefields

Beneath the pale moonlight glow,
A sea of frost begins to show.
The crystals dance on cold winds bright,
A silent realm of purest white.

A whisper soft, the night so still,
Each flake a dream, a ghostly thrill.
The world adorned in glistening lace,
Nature's touch, a frozen embrace.

Footprints left, in icy sheen,
A fleeting trace, a song unseen.
Echoed laughs in frosty air,
Moments caught, too bright to share.

A shimmer here, a gleam up high,
Stars twinkle in the velvet sky.
The icefields pulse with life concealed,
In dreams of warmth, their fate revealed.

Every breath, a cloud of white,
Caught in stillness, the heart ignites.
Through glimmering realms we wander far,
Guided softly by the northern star.

Serenade of the Silenced

In hushed woods where whispers fade,
Voices lost, their serenade.
Shadows linger, tales untold,
A melody of hearts grown cold.

Once bright songs, now quiet sighs,
Echo softly through the sighing pines.
Nature hums a solemn tune,
Beneath the watchful, waning moon.

From depths unseen, the shadows creep,
Among the lost, their secrets keep.
Serpentine paths, where hope once danced,
Now linger long, in silence entranced.

Fading laughter, a distant call,
Memories wrapped in time's cruel thrall.
Yet in the stillness, beauty hides,
A serenade where silence bides.

In every rustle, in every breeze,
The echoes blend with fading trees.
We listen close, though shadows veiled,
The serenade of souls unveiled.

Tundra Tales

Wide expanse of frozen land,
Stories lost beneath the strand.
Whispers carried by the chill,
Tales of courage, echoes still.

Across the stark and vibrant white,
Legends sleep in endless night.
Each scarred bough, each drifting snow,
Holds the secrets of long ago.

Footsteps brave through bitter winds,
Hearts aligned where fate begins.
Erosion speaks of time's fierce grip,
In the tundra's hold, we find our grip.

With every gust, the stories rise,
In frozen breath, the truth replies.
Whispers weave through icy trails,
On nature's stage, the heart unveils.

In quiet moments, wild and bare,
A tapestry of strength laid bare.
The tundra holds what time won't waste,
In every tale, a wisdom chaste.

Specters of Winter

Drifting shadows, white and gray,
Specters dance where children play.
Hushed the world in frosty breath,
Echoes linger, near to death.

Glimmers soft in twilight skies,
Transient forms of silent sighs.
Winter's ghosts in frosted trees,
Whisper secrets on the breeze.

Footprints trace paths of the past,
Moments fleeting, none will last.
Through the woods, the stories creep,
In the stillness, shadows weep.

Embers fade where fires were cast,
Winter's chill grips now so fast.
Memories cloaked in icy breath,
Serenade of life through death.

Yet amid the frost, there's light,
Every specter holds delight.
Whispers rise to greet the dawn,
In winter's heart, a new day drawn.

A Symphony of Stillness

In the hush of evening's glow,
Gentle whispers softly flow.
Stars above in silent dance,
Time slows down, a sweet romance.

Moonlight drapes the earth in peace,
All the noise begins to cease.
Nature holds its breath in grace,
In this moment, find your place.

Shadows stretch across the field,
In their arms, the world is healed.
Every heartbeat, every sigh,
Melodies beneath the sky.

Crickets play their nightly song,
In this symphony where we belong.
Close your eyes, drift into night,
In the stillness, feel the light.

Eclipsed by Snow

Silent flakes begin to fall,
Blankets wrap the earth in thrall.
Nature whispers, soft and low,
A world transformed, eclipsed by snow.

Trees wear coats of purest white,
In the calm of gentle night.
Footsteps muffled, quiet tread,
Where once was life, now dreams are fed.

Children laugh in winter's grace,
With rosy cheeks, they join the race.
Snowballs fly, a joyful show,
In the wonder, time can slow.

As dawn breaks with golden hue,
Sparkling light leads us anew.
In this moment, pure and bright,
Eclipsed by snow, hearts feel the light.

Frosty Mornings

Breath hangs heavy in the air,
Frosty patterns everywhere.
Sunlight breaks with gentle rays,
Kissing winter's cool embrace.

Fields lie still, a painted scene,
Nature's canvas, crisp and clean.
Birds awaken, chirp and glide,
In the morning, hearts collide.

A cup of warmth, the fingers cling,
Joy in every simple thing.
Laughter dances in the chill,
Frosty mornings, hearts to fill.

As shadows stretch and daylight grows,
Every moment softly glows.
Whispers of a day in store,
Frosty mornings, seek for more.

Secrets in the Silence

In the quiet, secrets hide,
Whispers carried on the tide.
Listen closely, heart awake,
In the stillness, truths may break.

Thoughts like rivers gently flow,
Bringing wisdom soft and slow.
Beneath the surface, layers deep,
In the silence, dreams will seep.

Moments linger, time unwinds,
In these spaces, clarity finds.
Voices echo, faint and clear,
In the silence, hold them dear.

Let your heart become the guide,
In the depths where dreams reside.
Secrets blossom, softly bloom,
In the silence, banish gloom.

Frosty Resilience

In the morning light, frost glistens,
Each crystal dances, softly listens.
Brittle branches stretch and sway,
Strength persists through winter's sway.

Amidst the chill, life finds a way,
Emerging blooms meet the light of day.
Against the cold, spirits grow bold,
Stories of warmth yet untold.

Silent whispers in the trees,
Hold secrets carried by the breeze.
Nature's pulse, beating bright,
Frosty resilience meets the night.

Every flake, a tale to weave,
In their splendor, we believe.
Through the freeze, the heart stays warm,
Love endures, a timeless charm.

As the seasons shift and change,
All the colors rearrange.
From frost to bloom, the cycle's call,
Life persists, and triumphs all.

Chasm of Cold

Beneath the moon, a valley yawns,
In the chasm where silence dawns.
Frozen winds howl through the night,
Echoes of dreams lost to sight.

Shadows dance in the pale glow,
Nature's blanket hides below.
A breath of frost, a shiver runs,
In the abyss where daylight shuns.

Stars above, a distant gleam,
In the darkness, a flickering dream.
Chill of silence, a deep embrace,
Wonders hidden in this space.

Branches heavy with snowflakes drift,
Time stands still, this is the gift.
Cold as ice, yet beauty lies,
In the cold grasp of winter skies.

Footprints mark where hearts have tread,
In the depths of white, whispers spread.
Love holds fast through bitter cold,
In the chasm, we remain bold.

Midnight Ice

Under the veil of midnight wide,
Crystal sheets on the river slide.
Stars reflected in shimmering glass,
In this stillness, moments pass.

Moonlight weaves a silver thread,
Over landscapes, gently spread.
Every shimmer, a story told,
In the heart of the night so cold.

Breath turns to mist, a fleeting sigh,
As the world dons a frosty tie.
Whispers echo through the dark,
Carried softly to each spark.

Frozen still, the night awaits,
Silent guards at nature's gates.
In this realm of ice and peace,
All worries cease, and hearts release.

Embrace the magic of the chill,
In midnight beauty, time stands still.
Through the dark, hope glistens bright,
In every shadow, there's a light.

Winterscape Wonder

A canvas stretched in hues of white,
Winterscape glows in gentle light.
Each flake a wonder, unique and true,
Painting the world in shades of blue.

Hushed are the sounds of life today,
As nature lies in a frosty sway.
Mountains draped in a soft embrace,
Hold the magic of this place.

Footsteps crunch on snow, a song,
In the chill where we belong.
Every breath releases glow,
Finding warmth in the wintry show.

Glistening paths, trails to explore,
Open wonders, forevermore.
Through the frost, our hearts collide,
In this beauty, we take pride.

As the seasons turn and blend,
Winterscape whispers, "I'll be your friend."
In every snowflake's silent fall,
Lies the wonder that connects us all.

Fragments of the Icy Spell

Whispers dance on frozen air,
Shimmering lights, a dream laid bare.
Crystal patterns weave and twine,
Nature's art, a mystic sign.

Beneath the surface, silence glows,
Hidden secrets, time bestows.
Glistening shards of moonlit night,
In each fragment, pure delight.

Snowflakes tumble, gentle kiss,
Each a promise, fleeting bliss.
In their fall, a tale is spun,
Fragments gather, one by one.

With every pause, the world stands still,
Echoes soft, the heart does thrill.
A fleeting glimpse of what may be,
In icy spells, we find the key.

Breathless in the Midst of Winter

Painted skies in shades of gray,
Winter's breath, a soft ballet.
Snowflakes fall, like whispers sweet,
Every flake at my feet.

Trees stand tall, their branches bare,
In the chill, memories flare.
Echoes of laughter, lost in time,
Breathless moments, pure and prime.

Frosty winds weave through the pines,
In this stillness, nature shines.
The world wrapped in a crystal cloak,
As if in dreams, we gently soak.

With every breath, a cloud appears,
Painting warmth amidst the fears.
In winter's heart, we find our place,
A breathless dance, a warm embrace.

The Cold Embrace

Underneath the silver sky,
A chilling grasp, no goodbye.
Frozen dreams and silent screams,
In this night, reality seems.

Winds that bite, a lover's touch,
Cold and harsh, yet holds us much.
In the stillness, shadows play,
The cold embrace won't fade away.

Icicles dangle, sharp and bright,
The heart beats slow in winter's plight.
Every moment seems to chill,
Yet in it all, a warmth does thrill.

Lurking beneath the icy lands,
Are whispers soft, like gentle hands.
In every breath, a secret lives,
The cold embrace, the heart forgives.

Reverberations of Ice

Echoes ring through winter's core,
Reverberations we can't ignore.
Cracking sounds beneath our feet,
Nature's tune is bittersweet.

Each shatter tells a story told,
Of countless winters, fierce and bold.
Beneath the layers, life goes on,
In icy realms, dusk till dawn.

Mountain peaks with frozen sighs,
Mirroring the quiet skies.
In the stillness, secrets keep,
Reverberations, deep and steep.

The heart beats slow, the world turns white,
In icy realms, we find our light.
With every sound, a memory wakes,
In reverberations, love still aches.

Enchanted by Crystal

In the twilight glow, so soft and bright,
A realm of wonder, a pure delight.
With whispers of magic in the air,
Crystal dreams shimmer everywhere.

A gentle breeze weaves through the trees,
Carrying songs with a soothing ease.
Each branch adorned with icy lace,
Nature's beauty, a sacred space.

The moonlight dances on the frozen stream,
Every glimmer like a fleeting dream.
Stars peek out from the velvet skies,
As night unfolds, the magic flies.

In moments still, the heart knows peace,
As worries fade, and troubles cease.
With every breath, a world reborn,
In crystal visions, a love sworn.

So linger here in this wondrous land,
Where dreams and reality gracefully stand.
For in each crystalline wonder we find,
The joys of life, forever entwined.

Secrets of the Snowfall

Beneath the quiet, a whisper flows,
As soft as feather, it gently glows.
Secrets hidden in the winter's breath,
A tale of wonder, a dance with death.

Snowflakes twirl in the flickering light,
Each one unique, a shimmering sight.
They carry messages from the past,
Of dreams and hopes that were meant to last.

The world wrapped in a blanket of white,
A canvas painted by the moon's light.
Silencing footsteps, a gentle hush,
Inviting hearts to pause and crush.

Underneath layers, life sleeps below,
Waiting for spring when flowers will grow.
In each falling flake, a secret lies,
A promise held in the winter skies.

So wander softly, and listen close,
To the secrets that the snowflakes propose.
For in their silence, life takes its turn,
A world in slumber, patiently yearn.

Silent Flurries

In a muted world, the flurries fall,
Dancing softly, they heed the call.
Gentle whispers, a tender song,
In silence, winter feels so strong.

Twisting and swirling, a playful breeze,
Each flake a story, carried with ease.
A hush envelops the sleeping earth,
Reminding us all of quiet worth.

Footprints vanish, like dreams at dawn,
As nature's canvas begins to fawn.
In the stillness, hearts start to soar,
Finding beauty in what comes before.

Frozen moments, captured in time,
A world transformed, a life sublime.
With every gust, new wonders appear,
In silent flurries, all feels so clear.

So let us cherish this fleeting grace,
And embrace the stillness of winter's face.
For in each flurry, a blessing we see,
A reminder of life's simplicity.

The Stillness Between

In the pause of twilight, soft and sweet,
Life finds a moment, calm and complete.
With shadows stretching, daylight fades,
Whispers of peace in the evening glades.

Between the heartbeats, silence dwells,
A gentle echo, like ringing bells.
In every breath, we feel the grace,
Of stillness wrapped in a warm embrace.

Stars appear, twinkling high above,
In the quiet, we find our love.
For in that space, where time holds fast,
Memories linger, shadows cast.

As night unfolds, and dreams arise,
In the stillness, truth never lies.
Tender moments, woven tight,
In the silence, we find our light.

So cherish the stillness, let it reside,
Where hearts converge and dreams abide.
For in the space that time forgot,
Life's sweetest treasures, they linger a lot.

Harmony in the Cold

Whispers dance on frosty air,
Nature sings, a tender prayer.
Branches draped in crystal lace,
Silent beauty, a frozen grace.

Footsteps crunch on snowy ground,
Where peace in stillness can be found.
In hushed tones, the world awakes,
A symphony the silence makes.

Gentle flurries start to twirl,
As winter's breath begins to swirl.
Textures blend, a canvas bright,
In harmony, both day and night.

Cold embraces every sound,
With warmth that lingers all around.
Hearts unite in softest glow,
Together in this world of snow.

From frosty morn to dusk's retreat,
The pulse of life, a rhythmic beat.
In winterscape, we find our song,
In this cold, we all belong.

Spirals of White

Flakes descend in tender spirals,
As winter weaves its white denials.
A dance of crystals in the sky,
Softly drifting, floating high.

Each tiny flake, a story told,
A journey new, a journey old.
Together they create a sea,
Of glistening calm, a tapestry.

Patterns swirl, the winds conspire,
In every gust, a subtle fire.
They twirl and play in frosty air,
In winter's grasp, they find their fair.

Underneath this cover pure,
Lies hidden warmth, the heart's allure.
In spirals grand, the world unwinds,
A fleeting moment love defines.

With every breath, we find release,
In nature's art, we find our peace.
So let us dance in winter's light,
With hope and joy, in spirals bright.

Eons of Ice

Time carves out this frozen land,
With ancient touch of nature's hand.
Mountains rise, their peaks adorned,
In silence, history is formed.

Glaciers move, a silent might,
In measured pace, through day and night.
A world encased in icy dreams,
Where time is caught in chilly seams.

Echoes of eons softly call,
From shadows deep, where glacial thrall.
Twilight lingers, a ghostly breath,
In winter's womb, we greet our death.

Yet life persists beneath the chill,
With whispers of a gentle thrill.
Beneath the frost, a pulse alive,
Through eons, spirits strive to thrive.

In this expanse, we find our plight,
Reflecting stars in endless night.
Together here, we stand, we rise,
In eons past, we seek the skies.

Moonlit Icicles

Dormant dreams hang from the eaves,
In silver light, the world believes.
Icicles gleam like crystal swords,
Guardians of the night's accords.

Moonlit whispers fill the air,
With secrets known to few who dare.
Each drop of dew, a story weaved,
In icy strands, the night conceived.

Frosted edges catch the glow,
Where shadows dance, the night to show.
Shimmering chandeliers of frost,
Remind us of what's gained and lost.

Underneath this frozen frame,
The heart ignites the quiet flame.
In solitude, the magic grows,
Where love and light in darkness glows.

So let us wander through the night,
Beneath the stars, in pure delight.
In moonlit beams, we find our way,
With icicles as guides, we sway.

Iced Over Memories

Frozen whispers in the breeze,
Dusty dreams beneath the trees.
Shadows dance where warmth had played,
In time's embrace, our hearts delayed.

Fragments glisten in the haze,
Echoes lost in winter's gaze.
Thoughts like snowflakes drift apart,
Chilling softly in the heart.

Silent nights, the stars collide,
In cold corners, memories hide.
Each one etched with frost's caress,
A haunting, sweet, and cold distress.

Candles flicker, shadows stir,
In the stillness, feelings blur.
Moments caught in icy chains,
Whispered names, like soft refrains.

Lost in time, yet crystal clear,
I hold tightly to what's dear.
Through the frost, I seek the light,
In my heart, the flame ignites.

Serene Snowfall

Gently drifts the silver white,
Blanketing the world in night.
Whispers soft as quilted dreams,
Stars reflect in quiet streams.

Each flake falls, a story told,
Woven warmth against the cold.
Silence reigns in this embrace,
Nature's slow and tender grace.

Footprints trace a quiet path,
In the stillness, peace we grasp.
Every breath, a misty sigh,
Underneath the velvet sky.

Branches bow, adorned in lace,
Holding winter's soft embrace.
Lightly falling, hopes arise,
In this still, enchanting guise.

Winter's gift, a tranquil heart,
In the moments, worlds depart.
Lost in wonder, lost in time,
Nature's hymn, a simple rhyme.

Slumbering Wilderness

In the woods where shadows sleep,
Silent secrets, whispers deep.
Snowflakes cloak the ancient trees,
Breathing softly in the breeze.

Nature's quilt wraps earth so tight,
Stars gaze down, a watchful light.
Branches bow with gentle grace,
Holding tight a quiet space.

Among the pines, the stillness reigns,
Echoes drift like soft refrains.
Every rustle, every sigh,
Nature's lullaby nearby.

Moonlight bathes the frozen ground,
In this haven, peace is found.
Frozen streams reflect the sky,
In the calm, the heart can fly.

Slumbering echoes, wild and free,
Whisper tales of harmony.
In this world, both vast and close,
Dreams awaken, winter's prose.

Frigid Epiphanies

Chill of dawn, a thought takes flight,
Through the frost, a gleaming light.
In the stillness, truths appear,
Wrapped in ice, the mind draws near.

Moments pause, reflect the soul,
In the frozen, find the whole.
Every breath, a crystal clear,
Voices echo, ever near.

Wisdom blooms in icy ground,
In the vacuum, truths are found.
Silent sighs, a soft release,
In the cold, we find our peace.

Winter's breath brings clarity,
In the quiet, we can see.
Each epiphany like a star,
Guiding us, no matter how far.

Frigid nights inspire new day,
With each thought, we find our way.
Through the ice, our spirits rise,
In the stillness, wisdom lies.

Fragments of Frost

Whispers of winter, soft and light,
Crystal shards glimmer in the night.
Nature's breath catches, frozen air,
Moments of beauty so rare and fair.

Trees wear coats of glistening white,
Silent echoes of pure delight.
Every branch a story unfolds,
In glacial embrace, the silence holds.

Paths etched deep in a blanket of snow,
Footprints left where the cold winds blow.
Soft shadows dance in the early dawn,
A fleeting glimpse, then they are gone.

Colors fade to shades of gray,
As twilight brings the close of day.
Yet in the chill, warmth can be found,
In loves that linger, hearts unbound.

A World Adrift in Ice

You stand alone on the frozen lake,
Outlines blur in the chilling wake.
A canvas painted in cobalt blue,
As sky and water meld into view.

Whispers of dreams caught in the frost,
A silent beauty, yet not at cost.
The world is calm, a breath held tight,
In this kingdom of winter's light.

Bubbles trapped in a shimmering sheet,
Tiny wonders beneath your feet.
Mother Nature keeps her secrets close,
In this stillness, we cherish the most.

Time seems to halt in the ice-bound scene,
The pulse of the earth, so serene.
A world adrift, where moments freeze,
And hearts can throb with gentle ease.

Reflections in Winter's Mirror

Stillness surrounds, a deafening hush,
In winter's grasp, there's no need to rush.
Clouds mirror thoughts in a pale gray sky,
Where echoes of laughter seem to fly.

Frosted windows frame a winding glow,
As embers dance in their flickering show.
Stories are whispered by crackling flame,
Each detail etched, never the same.

Glistening branches adorned with snow,
Each crystal a fragment of time's flow.
A reflection cast in ice and light,
Where shadows linger, holding tight.

Dreams unfurl like drifting flakes,
Fleeting moments, the heart aches.
In the mirror of winter, we find our peace,
As the chill of the season brings sweet release.

The Chill of Distant Stars

In the depths of night, a shimmering sigh,
Stars waltz across the darkened sky.
They twinkle like whispers from worlds afar,
A chill that beckons from every star.

Time stretches thin in this cosmic sea,
Each pinprick of light holds infinity.
Galaxies swirl in a lover's embrace,
The chill of the cosmos, a tender trace.

Breathe in the silence of heavens wide,
Where mysteries linger, and secrets hide.
The chill runs deep through the void of space,
Yet warms the heart in this endless chase.

Under starlit skies, dreams take flight,
Dancing with shadows, lost in the night.
In the chill of distant stars, we roam,
Finding the universe can feel like home.

Frostbitten Memories

Wrapped in blankets, dreams encase,
Frozen whispers linger, trace.
Moments captured, crystal clear,
In the silence, I hold dear.

Snowflakes drift like lost old thoughts,
In the stillness, time is caught.
Winds of winter softly play,
Reminding me of yesterday.

Frost on windows, frosted breath,
Every second, echoes death.
Yet within the chill I find,
A warmth that sparks the heart and mind.

The hearth's glow, a flickering fire,
Lines of memory never tire.
Each laugh that dances through the night,
Makes the cold feel warm and bright.

In the shadows, past sleeps tight,
Locked away from morning light.
Yet I cherish each embrace,
Of frostbitten time, a gentle grace.

Echoes Beneath the Ice

Below the surface, whispers roam,
Trapped in silence, they call home.
Echoes of tales long forgotten,
In the stillness, voices cotton.

Crystals shimmer with a sheen,
Memories lost, yet still seen.
Bound in layers thick and cold,
Secrets of the past unfold.

Ripples form but never break,
Underneath, a heart could ache.
Caught in time, forever freeze,
A history woven through the freeze.

Every crack a story told,
Of dreams and hopes, young and old.
Beneath the weight, life does reside,
In shadows deep, where secrets hide.

As I tread on frozen ground,
A symphony awaits, profound.
With every step, I feel the chase,
Of echoes trapped in winter's embrace.

Winter's Veil

Blanketed in white so pure,
Winter's breath a calming cure.
Trees wear crowns of glistening frost,
In this beauty, we are lost.

Pine-scented air fills my lungs,
With nature's choir, soft songs sung.
Each flake whispers a silent tune,
Beneath the gaze of a silver moon.

In the stillness, shadows creep,
Froze in time, the world is deep.
Yet laughter breaks the icy hush,
In winter's arms, there's always a rush.

Children's footprints line the way,
In frosted fields, they jump and play.
The joy of snowflakes on the ground,
In every corner, love is found.

As night descends, the stars ignite,
Under winter's veil, pure delight.
In this serene, enchanting land,
We find the warmth of heaven's hand.

Dances of the Northern Lights

Colors twirl across the sky,
In a ballet, vibrant and spry.
Flashes of green, pink, blue and gold,
A timeless story, bright and bold.

Nature's joy blooms above the ice,
In shimmering waves, they entice.
The cold air crackles with delight,
As night unveils the cosmic light.

In awe, we stand, hearts in flight,
Under the canvas of starry night.
Each ripple, a dance, a silent song,
Whispering memories, where we belong.

The universe sways, a lover's waltz,
In the darkness, every heart exalts.
Magic sashays in the northern breeze,
A tapestry woven with graceful ease.

As dawn approaches, colors fade,
Yet the magic, forever stayed.
In dreams, the lights forever thrive,
With every heartbeat, they come alive.

Frozen Footprints

In the snow, prints disappear,
Silent whispers, soft and clear.
Nature's tale etched in white,
Journey spoken, day turns night.

With each step, the cold does bite,
Yet the path feels warm and bright.
Footsteps echo on the ground,
In this stillness, peace is found.

Underneath the silver moon,
Frosty winds begin to croon.
Memories dance like shadows fleet,
In the night, where heartbeats meet.

A fleeting moment, lost, then found,
Frozen dreams from eyes abound.
As time drifts, like snowflakes fall,
We embrace the stillness, the call.

With the dawn, the world awakes,
Revealing all the paths we take.
Though the footprints fade away,
In our hearts, they choose to stay.

Crystal Caverns

Deep in the earth where shadows play,
Crystal caverns light the way.
Reflections dance on walls of stone,
In silent beauty, I feel at home.

Stalactites hang like frozen tears,
Holding secrets through the years.
Whispers echo, tales of old,
In crystal realms, warm and cold.

Glowing gems in the dark embrace,
Time stands still in this hallowed space.
Each step draws me closer still,
To the heart of nature's will.

As cool waters trickle down,
Softly in the silence, I drown.
With each echo, a mystery sings,
In the caverns, the magic clings.

In this wonder, fears dissolve,
Facets of light, a heart to evolve.
Through the darkness, I find my way,
In these crystal caverns, I long to stay.

Glacial Passages

Winding paths of ice and snow,
Through the glacial world we go.
Ancient giants guard the way,
Whispering tales of cold decay.

Each breath a cloud, we tread with care,
In the stillness, the frosty air.
Nature's breath, a timeless chill,
In these passages, time stands still.

Blue hues shimmer, an icy sea,
Flowing through vast eternity.
Each corner turned, a new surprise,
Underneath the endless skies.

Footsteps echo, softly hum,
As nature's heart begins to drum.
With every pulse, the glaciers sing,
To the chill of the winter's ring.

Finding spark in the frigid light,
Guided by stars, through the night.
In the glacial realms, I roam free,
Lost in wonders yet to see.

Winter's Heartbeat

In quiet nights, the world turns white,
Winter's heartbeat, soft and light.
Flakes like whispers gently fall,
Nature's silence, a whispered call.

Frosty branches clutch the sky,
Underneath, the shadows lie.
With every breath, the cold invigorates,
In winter's arms, the magic waits.

Candles flicker, warming rooms,
Against the chill that softly looms.
Stories shared by hearthside glow,
In this season, love will grow.

Dances of snow in the twilight,
Painting landscapes, pure delight.
In every flurry, joy is found,
Winter's heartbeat wraps around.

As nights grow long and days retreat,
In the frosty world beneath my feet,
I find solace in the quiet spin,
In winter's heart, I breathe within.

Frozen Footprints

In the snow, a path is laid,
Silent steps, memories fade.
Each mark a story left behind,
Echoes of the heart and mind.

Crystals dance in the cold air,
Nature's beauty, stark and rare.
Footprints whisper tales of old,
In the silence, hearts unfold.

Winter's breath on frozen ground,
Life's a journey, lost and found.
With each step, we tread the past,
In the snow, our shadows cast.

Moonlit nights, reflections glow,
In the stillness, we all know.
Every footprint, every trace,
Time's embrace in a frozen space.

As the seasons come and go,
We move forward, through the snow.
With each change, new paths will rise,
Frozen footprints under skies.

Whispers of the Chilled Moon

Under the moon, a chill descends,
Whispers float, where night transcends.
Stars converse in twinkling light,
Secrets shared through velvet night.

Frosted leaves begin to sigh,
Beneath the gaze of the deep sky.
Nature murmurs, soft and clear,
In the stillness, we draw near.

Moonbeams lace the world in white,
A tapestry of pure delight.
Echoes of dreams in the night breeze,
Winter's charm brings us to ease.

Through the branches, shadows weave,
In this moment, we believe.
Every whisper, soft and low,
Guides us through the drifting snow.

As the night begins to fade,
The dawn breaks, the stars evade.
Yet the whispers hold their grace,
In the heart, they find their place.

Captive of Winter's Hand

In the frost, the world is bound,
Nature sleeps beneath the sound.
Winter wraps its arms so tight,
Holding dreams through the long night.

Icicles hang like fragile tears,
Each one cradles whispered fears.
A realm of silence, pure and vast,
Moments linger, shadows cast.

Firelight flickers in the gloom,
Against the chill, we find a room.
Warmth and comfort, side by side,
In this space, our hearts abide.

As morning light begins to play,
The frost recedes, but we will stay.
Captive in winter's gentle grasp,
Embraced by time, in dreams we clasp.

When spring arrives, we'll break our chains,
But winter's beauty still remains.
In our hearts, we'll hold the past,
A love for winter, unsurpassed.

Tides of Frost

The waves of frost kiss the shore,
Nature's breath, a chilling roar.
In the dusk, the tides retract,
Whispers of cold secrets intact.

Each flake a drop from winter's sea,
Dancing lightly, wild and free.
Frosty fingers trace the sand,
A fleeting touch, a season's hand.

As the moon pulls, it shapes the night,
Guiding stars with silver light.
The ocean's pulse beneath the freeze,
Nature's rhythm, weaves with ease.

Underneath the quiet sky,
Frosty waves will ebb and sigh.
In the change, a promise lies,
New beginnings 'neath clear skies.

And as the frost begins to fade,
Life returns, unafraid.
Yet in memory, we shall keep,
The tides of frost, in dreams, we leap.

Solstice Shadows

In the stillness of the night,
Shadows dance with whispered light,
Branches bare, a ghostly sheen,
Where the sun has never been.

Echoes of the fading sun,
Veils of darkness, softly spun,
Midnight winds a chilling breath,
Hiding warmth, embracing death.

Figures slip in twilight's hold,
Stories of the brave and bold,
Crickets sing their solemn song,
In this realm, where all belong.

Silent paths beneath the trees,
Carried forth by ghastly breeze,
Every step a whispered chance,
To join the shadows in their dance.

As the solstice mourns the day,
Night ascends, the light will sway,
Trust the dark to show the way,
Solstice shadows softly play.

Frosted Parables

On the window, patterns lace,
Winter's art, a frosted grace,
Each a tale of brisk delight,
In the glow of morning light.

Snowflakes whisper in the breeze,
Telling tales of ancient trees,
Wrapped in white, the world anew,
Frosted dreams that once we knew.

Icicles hang like frozen chimes,
Marking laughter, silent rhymes,
In the cold, a spark divine,
Frosted parables entwined.

Every step, a crunching sound,
Magic lingers all around,
Footprints leading where we've been,
Through the winter's silver sheen.

In the quiet, hearts take flight,
Wrapped in warmth against the night,
Stories written just for us,
Frosted parables we trust.

Lost in the Snowfall

Gentle flakes begin to fall,
Silence wraps the world in thrall,
Whispers soft like lullabies,
Dancing dreams beneath the skies.

Paths erased, horizons blend,
Every turn a found new end,
In this maze of white and gray,
Lost in the snowfall, we stay.

Footprints fading, trails unmade,
Nature's game, a sweet charade,
Windswept echoes call our names,
In the snow, we play our games.

Every drift a secret breath,
Timeless tales of life and death,
With each flake, a story spun,
In the quiet, we become one.

As we wander, hearts entwined,
In the snowfall, peace we find,
Lost but found in winter's hold,
Magic woven, dreams unfold.

Celestial Crystals

Stars cascade through velvet night,
Celestial crystals spark with light,
Dancing in the cosmic sea,
Whispers shared between the free.

Nebulas spin a dreamlike dance,
Galaxies in a cosmic trance,
In this vast, enchanting space,
Celestial wonders, pure embrace.

Every twinkle a silent song,
Echoes of the universe strong,
Holding secrets of the past,
In their glow, our dreams are cast.

Planets turn in graceful arcs,
Guided by the shimm'ring sparks,
Boundless love in every sight,
Celestial crystals, pure delight.

As we gaze into the night,
Finding joy in starlit light,
In their shimmer, hearts can soar,
Celestial dreams forevermore.

Elysium of the North

In the realm where whispers freeze,
Beneath the dance of ancient trees.
The sky a canvas, shades of white,
Draped in the soft embrace of night.

Stars twinkle like distant dreams,
Echoing with the moon's bright beams.
Snowflakes fall, a gentle kiss,
A haven found in winter's bliss.

Mountains crowned with icy lace,
In this stillness, time finds its place.
A silent symphony unfolds,
Tales of beauty, gently told.

Winds that weave through frosted airs,
Carrying secrets of empty snares.
Hearts aflame with winter's glow,
In Elysium, love's warmth does flow.

Amidst the beauty, life takes pause,
Embracing nature's tender laws.
Here in the North, spirit takes flight,
In the embrace of endless night.

Shards of Light and Cold

Across the ice, the shadows play,
Where sun and frost meet, hearts will sway.
A world of contrasts, bright and dim,
Each fragment glimmers on a whim.

Crystals form on branches bare,
A tapestry of beauty rare.
In the silence, echoes call,
Through glittering spaces, we stand tall.

Glimmers dance on every flake,
Whispers of warmth, the cold will shake.
Chilling air that bites and stings,
Yet in the frost, hope gently sings.

Moments caught in gleams of gray,
Reflecting dreams that drift away.
Yet in the shards, we find our way,
Light guiding through the wintry sway.

To dwell in this duality,
Is to embrace the clarity.
For in the cold, we learn to see,
The truest form of harmony.

Frost Flowers Bloom

In the stillness of the morn,
Frost flowers break the night's deep scorn.
Delicate petals, crystal bright,
Awake beneath the soft sunlight.

Each bloom a whisper, soft and pure,
Nature's art, an ancient cure.
They raise their heads to greet the day,
In shimmering hues, they softly sway.

A garden born from winter's breath,
Living beauty amidst the death.
Fragile lives that dare to thrive,
In the chill, they come alive.

Framed by cold, they make their stand,
Vibrant spots in a white-land.
In clusters bright, they share their grace,
A fleeting moment, a timeless place.

Frost flowers bloom, a quiet cheer,
In the heart of winter, crystal clear.
A reminder of life's gentle art,
That even in cold, warms the heart.

Chill Shadows

Flickering lights in the evening's sway,
Cast chill shadows in hues of gray.
Whispers linger in the fading light,
Through the dusk, they dance in flight.

Silhouettes play on walls of frost,
Memories echo of warmth now lost.
The air turns crisp as daylight fades,
In the chill, a magic invades.

Every corner, a story told,
In the hush of night, brave and bold.
Through breath of winter, dreams take shape,
Life's fleeting moments, we must scrape.

Ghostly figures drift away,
In the embrace of night's soft play.
Yet in their wake, a warmth remains,
In chill shadows, love still reigns.

Through the dark, we seek the light,
Finding solace in the night.
For even in shadows cast so stark,
Hope can ignite like a tiny spark.

Snowbound Solitude

In the silence of the night,
The flakes gently fall down,
Blanketing the world in white,
Wrapping up the town.

Lonely paths are softly marked,
Footprints fade away,
While shadows dance in the dark,
Where children used to play.

Trees wear coats of sparkling snow,
Their limbs bow low with grace,
Time stands still, a fleeting show,
In this peaceful place.

Fires crackle, whispers low,
Beneath a starry dome,
In the warmth, we find a glow,
In solitude, our home.

A moment's pause amidst the chill,
Nature's breath, so pure,
In snowbound realms, we find the will,
To endure, to endure.

Frosted Whispers

A hush settles over the ground,
As frost paints every tree,
Whispers of winter's beauty found,
In silence, you and me.

Glistening patterns weave and twine,
Across the windowpane,
Each breath fogs in a soft design,
Where cold meets warmth again.

The world feels small, yet vast,
Under blankets of stillness,
Memories of seasons past,
Are held in winter's thrill.

Voices of the wind sing low,
Carrying tales of old,
Snowflakes twirl in a gentle flow,
A dance of stories told.

Frosted whispers fill the air,
As dreams begin to form,
In this realm of magic, rare,
We nestle, safe and warm.

Hushed Terrain

The landscape muffles every sound,
In a blanket soft and deep,
Hushed terrain where peace is found,
Nature's lullabies we keep.

Mountains rise with silent grace,
Crowned with caps of snow,
In this tranquil, cold embrace,
Time drifts gently slow.

Footsteps crunch on frosted ground,
Echoes fill the air,
With every step, a magic sound,
Lost in winter's care.

Beneath the sky of soothing gray,
A canvas pure and bright,
In quiet moments, we shall stay,
Till stars are born from night.

Winter's breath, a soft refrain,
The world in white attire,
In this hushed, enchanted vein,
We wander, hearts on fire.

Arctic Embrace

Beneath the northern lights aglow,
Where icy caresses weave,
An arctic land, so bright, so slow,
In nature's arms, we cleave.

Glaciers stand like ancient kings,
Silent guardians of time,
Offering warmth in chilling flings,
Wrapped in winter's rhyme.

The horizon blushes at dawn's call,
Cerulean skies above,
In the sparkle of snow, we enthrall,
Embracing winter's love.

Each breath kissed by frosty air,
We wander through the freeze,
In this moment, free from care,
Lost in frozen peace.

In every glance, a beauty rare,
As dreams meet the expanse,
In arctic embrace, we declare,
Together in this dance.

Breath of the North Wind

Whispers glide on frosty air,
Drawing tales of land so rare.
Through the pines, a chill does weave,
Nature's breath, a sigh, reprieve.

Ice-kissed branches bow with grace,
In the twilight's soft embrace.
Silver stars begin to gleam,
Cloaked in winter's tranquil dream.

Echoes of a distant call,
Winds that dance, they rise and fall.
A shivering hush blankets all,
In the silence, we stand tall.

Crisp and fresh, the world anew,
Every layer kissed with dew.
Breath of North, a tale untold,
In its grip, the world feels bold.

Frozen streams and skies of gray,
Guide the heart on winter's way.
With each gust, we find our strength,
In the cold, we go to length.

Icy Lullabies

In the night, the snowflakes fall,
Whispers soft, they beckon all.
A lullaby of purest white,
Cradles dreams in silent night.

Moonlight glints on frosted ground,
Every heartbeat, hushed, profound.
Gentle flakes spin through the air,
Painting peace beyond compare.

Slumber deep, the world wrapped tight,
In this tranquil, starlit sight.
Icy hush, a soft embrace,
In this space, we find our place.

Harmonies of winter's song,
In their grasp, we all belong.
Melodies of flickering light,
Guide us through the velvet night.

Nestled warm, the fire glows,
Fables shared as the cool breeze blows.
Icy lullabies softly hum,
In our hearts, forever drum.

Shards of Light in Winter

Morning breaks with shards of light,
Frosted fields, a dazzling sight.
Ice crystals dance in sun's warm gaze,
Creating beauty, endless praise.

Every breath a cloud of steam,
In this world, we find our dream.
Nature's canvas, pure and bright,
Painting visions in the light.

Pine trees wear a coat of white,
Standing strong through day and night.
While winter's chill bites at our skin,
Hope and warmth still dwell within.

Glistening snow in diamond form,
Transforming earth into a norm.
Each ray bending soft and clear,
Shows us love is always near.

A beauty wrapped in cold's embrace,
Shards of light, a smiling face.
Through the starkness, joy will flow,
In winter's heart, our spirits grow.

Subzero Symphonies

Notes of winter, crisp and clear,
Subzero symphonies we hear.
Wind whistling through the barren trees,
Nature's orchestra hangs with ease.

Harmony of chill and grace,
In each flake, a tender trace.
Drifting softly to the ground,
In their fall, a magic found.

Frosty whispers play their tune,
Shimmering under silver moon.
Every breath, a note we sing,
To the cold, our praises ring.

Echoing through valleys deep,
Winter's music, love we keep.
With each heartbeat, rhythms burst,
In the frost, our souls immersed.

As the evening draws its veil,
Stillness reigns, a peaceful trail.
Subzero symphonies so bright,
Guide us gently into night.

Whispering Flakes

Falling soft, the snowflakes glide,
A dance of silence, nature's pride.
Each flake a secret, a whisper low,
In winter's breath, they drift and flow.

Lands adorned in purest white,
A canvas bright, a chill delight.
The world hushed, as if in prayer,
Embracing cold, with frosty air.

Trees stand tall, cloaked in sheen,
Branches bow with silver green.
Whispers travel on the breeze,
In snowy realms, hearts find ease.

Footsteps crunch in frozen lands,
Leaving traces like gentle hands.
Nature's art, a winter's tale,
In whispers, through the snow we sail.

Night descends, the moon aglow,
Casting shadows on the snow below.
A tranquil peace, a time to pause,
In whispering flakes, we find our cause.

Subzero Soliloquy

In the hush of frozen air,
Thoughts meander, light as prayer.
Voices echo, soft and clear,
A soliloquy, for hearts to hear.

Windows frost with icy lace,
Each breath a cloud, in this embrace.
Time stands still, in winter's glow,
Thoughts unfold like silent snow.

Reflections dance on frozen lakes,
Life in stillness, a pause it makes.
Whispers linger, lost in time,
Subzero tales, an endless rhyme.

Chills that wrap like a soft shawl,
In this stillness, we hear the call.
Moments stretch, as shadows play,
In solitude, we find our way.

The world outside, a crisp refrain,
Underneath, beats our quiet strain.
In subzero grace, we breathe and sigh,
Listening to the dreams that fly.

Ethereal Freeze

A realm of ice, where dreams reside,
In ethereal arms, we find our guide.
Stars above in silver nets,
In frozen whispers, our hearts are met.

Layers deep, the silence sings,
Winter's majesty, with curious wings.
Every breath, a feathered thought,
In chilly air, new wonders caught.

Bare branches reach for skies of gray,
While shadows play, in twilight's sway.
Cold kisses brush against our skin,
In this serene world, we breathe within.

The night unfolds, a gentle shroud,
Veiling secrets, wrapped in cloud.
A moment's grace suspended still,
In ethereal freeze, we feel the thrill.

So let the hush embrace and store,
The magic hidden at winter's core.
In the still, where wonders tease,
We dance along the ethereal freeze.

Frost's Gentle Kiss

Morning breaks with a tender glow,
Frost's gentle kiss begins to show.
Nature's diamonds on the ground,
In soft light, a beauty profound.

Fields of white and glistening trees,
Whispers stir in the waking breeze.
Each blade of grass wears a crown,
In winter's charm, the world slows down.

A carpet spread of icy lace,
On every surface, a delicate trace.
In this quiet, hearts entwine,
With frost's embrace, our spirits shine.

Clouds drift softly, painting the sky,
As birds flutter by, in the clear, high.
Life awakens beneath the chill,
With every breath, a peaceful thrill.

Beneath the frost, new dreams ignite,
As daylight dances, chasing the night.
In the stillness, joy persists,
Bathed in warmth from frost's gentle kiss.

A Canvas of Frost

The morning whispers soft and low,
A canvas dressed in diamond glow.
Each blade of grass, a crystal shard,
Nature's touch, a perfect guard.

Trees wear coats of icy lace,
In winter's grasp, a frozen space.
Footprints linger in the white,
Mapping tales of pure delight.

Sunrise glimmers, faint and rare,
Colors burst without a care.
Stillness holds the moment tight,
A fleeting dance of day and night.

Winds awaken, crisp and clear,
Whispers carried, soft and near.
In this realm of frost and chill,
Nature's peace, a tranquil thrill.

As day fades into dusk's embrace,
The stars arrive, a sparkling grace.
A canvas waits for night to claim,
In quiet beauty, still the same.

Twilights in Blue

Darkness dances with the light,
As day bows out, embracing night.
Skywears hues of deep despair,
Twilights whisper, secrets rare.

Shadows stretch, they yawn and sigh,
Paint the heavens, as dreams fly.
The moon peeks through the velvet sky,
With silver beams that softly cry.

Stars ignite with gentle spark,
Piercing through the velvet dark.
Each twinkle tells a timeless tale,
Of lovers' vows and ships that sail.

In the blue, a calm prevails,
Softening edges, soothing trails.
Echoes linger in the air,
Twilights catch a whispered prayer.

As night unfolds its tapestry,
Weaving shadows, setting free.
In this realm of serene hue,
Twilights blend the old and new.

Shivers of Light

Dawn breaks gently, a tender sigh,
Shimmers dance in the waking sky.
Golden rays kiss the cold ground,
In silence, warmth can be found.

Flickers chase the lingering dark,
Casting dreams like a vibrant spark.
Each beam whispers stories bright,
In the embrace of morning light.

Shadows scatter, fears take flight,
Hope is born with each new sight.
A canvas brushed with hues divine,
Shivers of light, a perfect sign.

As noon stretches, shadows grow,
Life awakens, a rhythmic flow.
In every corner, warmth ignites,
Beauty blooms in pure delights.

When dusk arrives, the colors fade,
But memories of light won't trade.
For every beam that kissed the day,
Shivers of light forever stay.

Frigid Flames

In winter's clutch, the flames take hold,
Frigid hearts defended, bold.
With crackling warmth that fills the air,
A flicker of love, a gentle glare.

Snowflakes fall, their dance so light,
Captured souls in the glowing night.
Embers sway in a fiery waltz,
Defying winter's cold, harsh faults.

Chasing shadows in amber light,
Frigid winds, they take flight.
Through the frost, the fire gleams,
Crafting warmth from shimmering dreams.

Every breath a cloud of white,
Lost in the magic, pure delight.
Together we brave the icy chill,
Frigid flames, love's perfect thrill.

As twilight fades to darker shades,
Together we face what fate parades.
The warmth within always remains,
In the dance of frigid flames.

Silent Frost

Morning glimmers, soft and pale,
A quiet world, the winds do wail.
Each breath a cloud, a fleeting ghost,
Silent frost, our thoughts engrossed.

Footsteps crunch on frozen ground,
Whispers of nature, tranquil sound.
Trees wear coats of icy lace,
In this stillness, I find my place.

Sunrise paints the sky anew,
With shades of pink and hints of blue.
Yet shadows linger, deep and vast,
Echoes of seasons, fading fast.

Frozen lakes, a mirrored dream,
Reflecting life—a silent theme.
In this realm, where time stands still,
The heart beats softly, calm and thrill.

As daylight wanes, the stars appear,
Magic lingers, ever near.
I embrace the night, wrapped in peace,
Silent frost brings sweet release.

Polar Enchantment

In the land where the snowflakes sing,
A world adorned, eternal spring.
Mountains loom, majestic, bright,
Polar enchantment, pure delight.

Whispers dance on frosty air,
A sparkling hymn, a love affair.
Crystals twinkle, a diamond sky,
In this wonder, we soar high.

Auroras waltz in colors bold,
Painting tales of myths untold.
Underneath their glowing gleam,
Dreamers wander, lost in dream.

Icicles hang, nature's art,
Framing moments, felt in heart.
Each flake a story, soft and bright,
Polar enchantment, a pure sight.

As twilight falls, the world transforms,
In a hush, the stillness warms.
Hand in hand, we find our way,
In this magic, forever stay.

Fractured Ice

Cracks appear on frozen lakes,
Whispers of change, the silence breaks.
Waves of color, deep below,
Fractured ice, a tale to show.

Beneath the surface, stories lie,
Of ages past, of time gone by.
Yet beauty lingers in decay,
Fractured ice finds a way to play.

The sun's warm glare, a gentle tease,
Melting dreams with a sighing breeze.
Nature's art, both rich and stark,
In every shard, a lasting mark.

With each shift, a crack resounds,
Life unfurls with tender sounds.
Through the fractures, hope may rise,
In broken paths, the spirit flies.

As seasons turn, we watch it gleam,
Fractured ice, a rebel's dream.
In its fragments, beauty finds,
A masterpiece that gently binds.

Whiteout Whispers

Snow envelops the world outside,
In a blanket where shadows hide.
Voices muted, echoes lost,
Whiteout whispers, nature's frost.

The landscape fades to shades of white,
A soft embrace, both pure and bright.
Footprints vanish without a trace,
In this silence, we find grace.

Softly falling, flakes descend,
Time suspended, moments blend.
Winter's hush, a sacred balm,
In the stillness, hearts feel calm.

Trees stand tall in snow's embrace,
Guardians of this tranquil space.
While the world slows, we move near,
In whiteout whispers, love draws near.

As night descends, the stars align,
A twinkling quilt, a cosmic design.
In frozen dreams and glowing light,
Whiteout whispers take their flight.

Shivering Silence

In the night's embrace, shadows creep,
Whispers of winter, secrets keep.
The frost clings tight, as stillness takes hold,
A world wrapped in dreams, silent and cold.

Moonlight dances on the frozen ground,
Heartbeats echo, no other sound.
Stars twinkle softly, in velvet skies,
Lost in the silence, where the heart lies.

Breath hangs like clouds, in the frigid air,
Alone in the night, wrapped in despair.
Yet beauty lingers in this quiet space,
A moment of peace, an endless grace.

The trees stand tall, cloaked in white,
Guardians of secrets, lost to the night.
In shivering silence, the world stands still,
A muted promise, nature's will.

As dawn approaches, the darkness recedes,
Fleeting shadows, as sunlight feeds.
But the silence remains, deep within,
A haunting melody, where dreams begin.

Crystal Threads

Threaded with light, the dawn reveals,
Crystal formations, spun like wheels.
Each droplet glistens, a world caught tight,
Nature's weave sings, in morning light.

Frosted branches, lace on trees,
Whispering tales in the gentle breeze.
A tapestry glows, soft and pale,
A shimmer of dreams, a delicate trail.

The sun breaks through, casting warm rays,
Golden reflections dance and play.
With every breath, life starts anew,
In this crystal world, every hue.

Nature's fabric, a wondrous art,
Stitched with beauty, it warms the heart.
Each thread entwined, a story told,
In every shimmer, mysteries unfold.

As day takes flight, the crystals fade,
Yet in our hearts, their beauty stayed.
For in every moment, the magic spreads,
Through the crystal threads, where wonder treads.

Frigid Symphony

A symphony plays in the frosty air,
Notes of silence, sharply fair.
Ice-rimmed melodies drift and sway,
In the stillness, the music plays.

Each flake that falls is a quiet sound,
An orchestra bound, all around.
Strings of the wind weave through the trees,
Harmony flows with each chilling breeze.

The world enshrined in a frozen song,
Echoes of winter, sweet and strong.
With every gust, the whispers call,
A frigid overture that enchants us all.

As night descends, the stars align,
Notes of the cosmos, perfectly fine.
A celestial concert, vast and bright,
Guiding our hearts through the cold night.

Yet within this chill, a warmth will spark,
For in frigid symphonies, love leaves its mark.
In shared admiration, together we stand,
Listening close, hand in hand.

Snowbound Reverie

Lost in the drifts, a dream unfolds,
A winter's tale, in whispers told.
Snow blankets dreams in soft repose,
A snowbound reverie, where magic grows.

Footsteps vanish, under layers deep,
In this quiet world, the heart will leap.
Wonder awakes, as spirits soar,
In the embrace of winter, we explore.

Icicles dangle, like crystal tears,
Reflecting laughter, blurring fears.
With every flake, a whisper of hope,
We journey together, learning to cope.

As dusk settles, the sky ignites,
Stars shimmer down, a tapestry bright.
Together we wander, hand in hand,
In a snowbound reverie, so grand.

And when the dawn breaks, in hues divine,
We carry the magic, hearts entwined.
For in winter's grasp, we find our way,
In snowbound dreams, forever we stay.

Shadowed Under Snow

Whispers of winter, soft and light,
Branches bow low, cloaked in white.
Silence blankets the sleeping ground,
Secrets of nature, so profound.

Footsteps muffled, a careful tread,
Dreams hibernate, while the world is spread.
Each flake a story, kissed by the breeze,
Frozen moments, time's sweet tease.

Beneath the surface, life abounds,
Hidden rhythms, silent sounds.
The world breathes slow, in quiet grace,
Nature's beauty, our hearts embrace.

In twilight's glow, shadows play,
Glimmers of dusk, fading gray.
Snowflakes gather, a gentle sigh,
Under the moon, they dance and fly.

Eclipsed by stars, the night unfolds,
Stories of warmth, in winter cold.
Embers of life in a crystal shroud,
Forever cherished, forever loud.

Frost-kissed Horizons

Awake to dawn's breath, crisp and clear,
Morning light paints the world sincere.
Frost-kissed edges of blades and leaves,
Nature's palette, the heart believes.

Rivers glisten with a pearly sheen,
Reflecting whispers of the unseen.
Branches adorned in shimmering lace,
Winter's charm in a fleeting grace.

The horizon stretches, a canvas wide,
Beneath a blanket, the warmth does hide.
Clouds like brushstrokes, soft and bright,
Promise of journeys in fading light.

In the distance, mountains stand tall,
Guardians of secrets, ancient call.
Frosty breaths carry tales untold,
Echoing legends of brave and bold.

Through valleys deep where shadows creep,
Frost-kissed dreams lull the world to sleep.
Awakening springs accompany fate,
Fading winter as new blooms await.

Solstice Reverberations

Solstice whispers through the trees,
Bring forth warmth on the chilling breeze.
Days that linger, dance and play,
Casting shadows in bright array.

Crimson skies drape the twilight hour,
Radiant beauty, nature's power.
Echoes of laughter in the air,
Moments of joy, beyond compare.

Stars awaken in the velvet night,
Guiding dreams with their soft light.
Seasons shift, a gentle sigh,
Life renews as time sweeps by.

Ceremonies of light ignite,
In hearts of those who dare to fight.
Celebrations uniting the souls,
Under the heavens, each spirit extols.

As shadows blend with the glow of dawn,
Hope emerges, the night withdrawn.
In this symphony, life reverberates,
Solstice blessings, love translates.

Pathways of the Icebound

Crystalline trails stretch far and wide,
Footprints lined in the snow's white tide.
Pathways carved by unseen hands,
Guiding wanderers across the lands.

Frozen rivers whisper tales of yore,
Memories captured, forevermore.
Nature's canvas, in frosty hue,
Echoes of life, both old and new.

Beneath the frost, the earth lies still,
Holding its breath, awaiting thrill.
Echoed laughter dances on the air,
Moments of magic, beyond compare.

Over valleys where shadows wane,
Bridges of ice that hold the strain.
In every crack and crevice deep,
Lie dreams of yesteryears to keep.

Journey on these paths we weave,
In winter's grasp, we still believe.
Through frozen whispers, life's thread binds,
In pathways of the icebound finds.

Glaciers Whisper

Silent giants drift and sway,
Whispers carried far away,
Tales of time in icy flows,
Secrets only nature knows.

Shimmering blue in sunlit grace,
Eroding slowly, leaves no trace,
Frozen memories, ancient lore,
In their depths, we seek much more.

Cracks and creaks echo their song,
Majestic forms, forever strong,
Guardians of a changing land,
Holding truths we all demand.

Winter's breath upon their face,
Cloaked in frost, a perfect space,
Each slab a story yet untold,
In icy silence, brave and bold.

Journey forward, realm so vast,
Through the stillness, dreams held fast,
Glaciers whisper to the sky,
In their shadows, we learn to fly.

Chilling Embrace

Wrapped in winter's coldest breath,
A silent vow, a dance with death,
Frosted whispers in the night,
Nature's chill, a pure delight.

Branches bowed with heavy snow,
In the dark, a soft glow,
Stars twinkle in the frozen air,
Casting light on dreams laid bare.

Night descends, a velvet cloak,
Comfort found in midnight's smoke,
Every breath a cloud of white,
In this stillness, hearts ignite.

In the quiet, time stands still,
Winter's magic, pure and chill,
Embrace the cold, the tranquil peace,
In this moment, fears will cease.

Chilling echoes, softly hum,
Feel the pulse, the rhythm come,
In the frost, a warmth we find,
Chilling embrace, forever kind.

Frostbitten Dreams

In the stillness of the night,
Frostbite whispers, cold and bright,
Every breath a crystal shard,
Dreams wrapped tight, forever guard.

Moonlight dances on the snow,
Warming hearts with silver glow,
Winter wonders, dreams take flight,
Frostbitten visions, pure delight.

Footprints trace where shadows play,
Echoes fade of yesterday,
Wrapped in layers, soft and warm,
Through the cold, we weather the storm.

Winter's chill, a gentle song,
In its grasp, we all belong,
Frostbitten dreams, a sweet refrain,
In the quiet, beauty reigns.

Hold them close, these thoughts serene,
In the frost, a world unseen,
Fragile wishes, tender and bright,
With each dawn, they take their flight.

Icy Breath of Winter

With every gust, the cold winds play,
Icy breath asserts its sway,
Nature's chill wraps tight and fierce,
In its grasp, our hearts it pierce.

Frosted skies, a canvas grey,
Painting whispers, night and day,
Every flake a story told,
In this realm, we brave the cold.

Crystalline structures, sharp and pure,
In their beauty, we endure,
Winter's grasp, both harsh and kind,
Leaves us yearning, hearts entwined.

Underneath the blanket white,
Magic stirs in frozen light,
Icy breath weaves tales so grand,
Binding dreams across the land.

Seasons turn, yet still we feel,
Winter's breath, a sacred seal,
In the silence, we find peace,
Icy whispers that never cease.

Tundra's Lullaby

In the hush of evening's glow,
Whispers dance on winds that flow.
Blankets white on crystal ground,
Nature's calm, a soothing sound.

Stars like diamonds gently gleam,
Frosted branches softly team.
Moonlight spills on silent seas,
Tundra sings with winsome ease.

Beneath the vast, unending sky,
Snowflakes twirl, they drift and fly.
Every breath in cold air sweet,
Nature's rhythm, pure and neat.

Wolves in distance softly howl,
Cradled dreams as shadows prowl.
In this night, we find our peace,
Tundra's song, a warm release.

Close your eyes and hear the call,
Of the wild, embracing all.
In the stillness, hearts will sway,
Tundra's lullaby at play.

Shard of Stillness

In the depths of frozen lands,
Silence falls like gentle hands.
Crystal shards of twilight gleam,
Nature's breath, a quiet dream.

Hidden paths in frosted air,
Whispers of a world so rare.
Every echo softly stays,
Frozen echoes through the maze.

Icicles hang, a silent choir,
Reflecting light, a soft desire.
Stillness woven, threads of night,
Captured peace in silver light.

Time stands still in icy grace,
Mirrored moments we embrace.
In a world of quiet hues,
Shard of stillness, calm imbues.

Wrapped in layers, life unfolds,
Tales of winter softly told.
In each breath, a secret lies,
Glimmers bright beneath the skies.

Hushed Echoes of Ice

Crystals form where silence treads,
In the cold, where nature spreads.
Hushed echoes brush the icy stone,
Whispers linger, softly blown.

Underneath the northern lights,
Shadows dance on frosty nights.
Every step, a tender trace,
Marking life in nature's grace.

Beneath the weight of winter's sigh,
Time feels soft, as moments fly.
In the stillness, hearts collide,
Hushed echoes by our side.

Through the night, the world will sing,
Of the calm that cold can bring.
Every breath, a sacred peace,
In the quiet, fears release.

Icebound dreams in moonlit haze,
Twinkling stars, a silent praise.
In this realm of soft embrace,
Hushed echoes find their place.

Frosted Horizons

Where the sky meets icy ground,
Frosted horizons stretch around.
Whispers of a world so bright,
Shining softly in the night.

Every flake a story told,
Each a jewel, a sight to behold.
Winds of winter, fierce and free,
Kissing earth with gentle glee.

Through the mist, horizons gleam,
Painting landscapes like a dream.
Colors blend in frosted air,
Beauty found everywhere.

In the silence, peace bestowed,
Every path a secret road.
Frosted whispers guide the way,
To the dawn of a new day.

Hold the moment, breathe it in,
Let the magic now begin.
In this space where dreams reside,
Frosted horizons, hearts abide.

Chill of the Night Sky

Stars whisper softly, a tale in the dark,
Moonlight dances, igniting a spark.
Cold winds embrace all dreams taking flight,
In the quiet expanse of the chill of the night.

Shadows stretch long, under luminous glow,
Each twinkling beacon, a secret to know.
The world holds its breath, wrapped in delight,
As night unfolds softly, a blanket so tight.

Whispers of starlight weave through the trees,
Carried on breezes, they hum gentle pleas.
In each breath of evening, time slows to invite,
A serenade beckons, the chill of the night.

Glimmers and glances, the universe sings,
In voids full of wonder, our imaginations take wings.
Float along softly, let dreams take their height,
Embraced by the magic, the chill of the night.

When dawn gently breaks, the stars will retreat,
But memories linger, so tender and sweet.
In the heart of the cosmos, we find pure delight,
Forever enchanted by the chill of the night.

The Slumbering Earth

Beneath the soft blanket, the earth lies still,
Nature is sleeping, under winter's chill.
Branches are barren, yet promise anew,
In the cradle of silence, life whispers through.

Frost coats the meadows, a shimmering lace,
A stillness envelops, a tranquil embrace.
The heartbeat of nature, so steady and slow,
In the depths of the night, where dreams gently flow.

Mountains stand watch, bathed in moon's glow,
Guardians of secrets that only they know.
In the hush of the night, hopes softly unfurl,
Wrapped in serenity, the slumbering world.

Rivers whisper softly, frozen in time,
Cascading stillness, a lullaby rhyme.
Nature holds close, a treasure to unfurl,
In the gentle embrace of the slumbering world.

As the sun journeys forth, casting shadows wide,
Awakening nature, with arms open wide.
Yet in the twilight, as daylight's unfurled,
Rest easy in dreams of the slumbering world.

Glistening Veils of White

Snowflakes flutter down, each one a surprise,
Draping the landscape, a soft lullaby.
Fields dressed in white, so pure and so bright,
Whispers of winter, glistening veils of white.

Trees wear their crowns, of shimmering frost,
In beauty so fleeting, yet never lost.
The world holds its breath, in soft, silent light,
Embracing the magic, glistening veils of white.

Footsteps crunch lightly on the blanket below,
A dance with no rhythm, just winter's soft flow.
In the hush of the evening, there's peace in the sight,
A canvas of dreams, glistening veils of white.

Night's gentle touch brings a world of delight,
Stars peek through clouds, a silvery sight.
In the chill of the air, hearts are alight,
In the charm of the night, glistening veils of white.

As dawn paints the sky, hues of orange and gold,
Still linger the memories, quiet and bold.
In the heart of winter, where magic takes flight,
Forever enchanted by glistening veils of white.

Winter's Gentle Grip

Frost creeps in gently, whispering low,
Veils of soft silence blanket the snow.
Time slows to a waltz, under stars that drip,
A delicate dance in winter's gentle grip.

Pines stand like sentinels, cloaked in pure white,
Guarding the secrets of long winter nights.
Nature holds memories, shadows that slip,
Into the warm solace of winter's gentle grip.

Each flake a soft promise, as dreams intertwine,
In the heart of the cold, there's warmth so divine.
Wrapped in a world where frost seems to sip,
The beauty unfolds in winter's gentle grip.

Candles flicker softly, in homes filled with cheer,
Gathering 'round hearths as loved ones draw near.
With laughter and stories, hearts rise and dip,
In the warmth of the moments in winter's gentle grip.

As spring approaches, with whispers of light,
The frost will retreat from the softening night.
Yet memories linger, like ink on a script,
Forever we treasure winter's gentle grip.

Icebound Reverie

In silence deep, where shadows play,
Frozen dreams begin to sway.
Soft whispers dance on chilly air,
Lost in thoughts, without a care.

Snowflakes twirl in gentle flight,
Cloaked in white, the world feels right.
Time stands still, a crystal veil,
In this realm, we will not fail.

Glimmers shine like stars above,
Nature's touch, it speaks of love.
Through the chill, our spirits rise,
Boundless skies, no need for lies.

Branches heavy, laden with frost,
In this beauty, we find no cost.
Each heartbeat echoes in the snow,
A tranquil pulse, a soft aglow.

Together here, we share our thoughts,
In this winter, all else is naught.
With whispered dreams that softly blend,
In icebound reverie, we transcend.

Crystalized Echoes

A world transformed, so pure and bright,
In icy shards, the sun ignites.
Each breath we take, a frosty sigh,
In crystal dreams, we wander by.

Structures built from frozen tears,
Echoes of long-forgotten years.
Quiet moments, ethereal glow,
We lose ourselves in the soft snow.

Beneath the frost, our secrets lie,
In shimmering strands, they cannot die.
Truths unfold in a hidden light,
In crystalized echoes, hearts take flight.

Nature's art, a sculptor's touch,
Each frozen frame reveals so much.
Whispers of winter, vast and wide,
Together here, we shall abide.

In this stillness, we find our peace,
As worries fade, our spirits cease.
In the calm, we let love flow,
In crystalized echoes, we'll grow.

Glacial Heartbeats

In glaciers deep, where time stands still,
A rhythmic pulse, a tender thrill.
Each heartbeat echoes through the ice,
In frozen realms, we feel it twice.

Gentle whispers in the creaking cold,
Stories of ages, yet untold.
With every layer, history lies,
In glacial heartbeats, wisdom cries.

The world transforms, a muted hue,
As tides of winter draw us through.
We find the warmth in a chilling breeze,
In this embrace, we find our ease.

Footsteps crunch on a snowy lane,
Each stride a gift, no hint of pain.
As heartbeats sync beneath the sky,
In glacial rhythms, we will fly.

Together bound, through storms we chase,
In glacial heartbeats, we find our place.
A language soft, in quiet sighs,
In winter's grasp, our love won't die.

Frigid Landscapes Unfurled

A canvas wide, in shades of white,
Frigid landscapes bask in light.
Mountains rise, their peaks aglow,
In this domain, our spirits flow.

Icy rivers carve their path,
Balanced stillness in nature's math.
Snowy valleys, vast and grand,
In stillness, together we stand.

We wander through the frosted trees,
With frozen breath, we catch the breeze.
The world adorned, so pure, serene,
In frigid landscapes, love feels keen.

Distant echoes of winter's call,
Embrace the chill, let barriers fall.
As horizons stretch beyond our sight,
In frozen beauty, we find our light.

With each step, hearts intertwine,
In the cold, our warmth will shine.
Through the landscapes, mesmerized,
In frigid views, we are prized.

Veil of White

Snowflakes dance in the frosty air,
Blanketing the world with tender care.
Whispers of winter in the pale moonlight,
Gentle and soft, a pure, cold sight.

Trees stand still in their frozen grace,
Embraced by silence in this silent space.
Footsteps echo on the path so bright,
Guided by stars, a celestial flight.

Under the veil, the earth lies asleep,
Secrets of seasons buried deep.
Time stands still in this tranquil scene,
Wrapped in white, a cotton dream.

Breezes murmur through branches bare,
Carrying whispers of the forest's prayer.
Each flake a promise, unique and rare,
In winter's embrace, we find our share.

As dawn awakens with gentle light,
Colors emerge from the veil of white.
A world renewed, fresh hopes take flight,
In the quiet morn, all feels right.

Chill of Forgotten Dreams

In shadows cast by a fading light,
Dreams linger softly, out of sight.
Whispers carried on the evening breeze,
Tales of lost hopes among the trees.

Memories dance like ghosts in the night,
Flickering softly, dim and slight.
Each breath a story, each sigh a tale,
Of wishes unspoken, a heart left pale.

Stars above shine with distant gleams,
Reflecting the chill of forgotten dreams.
Time drifts slowly, a river wide,
Carrying thoughts, an unwavering tide.

In the stillness, echoes collide,
Faded emotions we try to hide.
Yet in the silence, hope can arise,
From the ashes of dreams that touch the skies.

Awake the heart with every new dawn,
Let go of the past, carry on.
For even in shadows, light will beam,
Awakening life from forgotten dreams.

Whispering Frost

In the still of night, the frost descends,
Covering the ground where daylight ends.
A glimmering veil on the world below,
Whispers of winter in the midnight glow.

Each blade of grass, a crystal spear,
Hushed secrets linger, quiet and clear.
While moonlight bathes the silent gleam,
Nature breathes softly as if in a dream.

Footsteps freeze on the frozen ground,
Echoes of silence, no other sound.
In the heart of winter, mysteries dwell,
Tales of the frost that the night can tell.

Under the stars, where shadows creep,
Whispers of frost in the silence deep.
A world transformed, so still and bright,
Cradled gently by the arms of night.

In the cool embrace, dreams intertwine,
With the thaw of spring, new paths align.
Yet for this moment, let stillness host,
The beauty that lies in whispering frost.

Shimmering Silence

In the twilight's glow, where shadows blend,
An air of magic seems to suspend.
With every flicker, the stars align,
Creating a canvas where silence shines.

Crickets sing their soft, gentle tune,
Praising the beauty of the silver moon.
A gentle breeze carries secrets untold,
In the shimmering silence, our hearts unfold.

Every moment breathes a tranquil sigh,
Under the vastness of the darkened sky.
Lost in the stillness, we find our space,
Embraced by the night in its warm embrace.

Reflections sparkle on the surface near,
Mirroring dreams that are precious and dear.
In the hush of the night, our spirits take flight,
Dancing with echoes in the soft moonlight.

In shimmering silence, thoughts intertwine,
Creating a tapestry we've defined.
As the world sleeps, let the night unfurl,
Embracing life's wonders in a silent swirl.

Milton Keynes UK
Ingram Content Group UK Ltd.
UKHW010231111224
452348UK00011B/676